THE PARADOX OF SONDER

JACK DUNBAR

authorHOUSE®

AuthorHouse™
1663 Liberty Drive
Bloomington, IN 47403
www.authorhouse.com
Phone: 833-262-8899

Published by AuthorHouse 05/22/2021

ISBN: 978-1-6655-2619-7 (sc)
ISBN: 978-1-6655-2617-3 (hc)
ISBN: 978-1-6655-2618-0 (e)

Library of Congress Control Number: 2021910151

For my family

Ne Te Quæsiveris Extra

Ut Cognoscant Te

Poetry

My Bounty

Silent Sighs

―――――

Oh you,
whose form is constant perils of my mind—
How must I bare the frankness of our silent sighs,
where eyes meet eyes, in longing stares do trial mine.

The Place Between Pages

———

Your wrist bends awkwardly
under your chin, as your eyes rub their
perfect pupils over the pages of the book
in your hand. Someone is cleaning in the
next room, banging pots in the kitchen sink.
In here is only the sound of your concentration
beside me on the couch, and me neglecting mine—
creating a far better story that I hope never ends.

To Catch You in its Arms

———

I was told of the science of tides once.
Of the moon,
up there in her quiet, lonely heavens,
making the waves throw themselves onto the sand.
Retreating, then gaining speed again and hurling themselves
onto an immovable shore, forever.
Their foamy fingers reach with every facet of their strength,
when flat on their stomach they're dragged back into the sea.

But science can be meager.
I know a different truth. Its origin: adoration.
The polar ice caps disappear into the water
and the waves inhale larger breaths inland,
not from the heat of the sun or the gaze of the moon,
but that the ocean might crawl further up onto the continents
to catch you in its arms.

At the Heels of an Olive Tree

———

Are you some risen god from ancient times, revitalized?
You provoke a riot in my tingling veins.
So wild and ever shameless.
Come feel a revolution and how it overthrows my senses!
Give your hand my chest and touch me familiar.
Oh, please— somehow purge me of this
incessant desperation to know you on the
deepest
human
level!
That I may understand your mind, if blind,
and where you lay, come nightfall.

What is this weakness unveiled in your body?
Why does my tongue refuse to get over its stage fright?
A wide, Apollonian back.
Your two and tensing hands. Tools of an Empire.
Turn this way, that I might see your face
and know my purpose, grey-eyed Athena.
Please glance at me just once, oh eyes of Medusa, that I may
turn to stone and never live another day without you being mine—
but stay here, frozen, in my granite admiration.

To See my Subtle Rescue

———

Shall we navigate uncharted waters?
You and me together, exploring.
I'll be the Captain; you be first mate.
Or the first mate as me, if you'd rather.
I've no skill in sailing, but I know the ocean well.
As boundless and as boisterous as she is.

And to imagine the thrill of finally yelling
to all the shipmates
                below,
after so long adrift the sea:
"Land Ho!"

Oh, to boldly shout my love the same.

Black Housefly

———

Our memories are the housefly in my apartment.
Fat.
Juicy.
Loud.
Nostalgia buzzes around, unconcerned.
I dwell on you often—
The fly loops around my head while I brush my teeth.
Sometimes I think about us randomly while I'm doing chores—
The fly is stuck beneath the lampshade in the dining room.

One spring afternoon, I have the window open to let a breeze in.
The vinyl screen shakes as the fly thuds against it.
I walk over and close the window.

Chisel

———

I sense the work you've done on me—
and doing still.
Meticulous. Planned out.
But every sense of reckless too—
The ting of the metal pick
under my armpit.
My calves are sanded to swollen
desert hillsides.
The arch of my elbows
streamline into forearms curving.
You softly blow at the sand
between my toes and
use a brush to clear away debris.
I am your masterpiece transfigured—
and will last for a thousand years.

Ironing a Shirt Before Work

———

Loving you is
ironing a shirt before work.
In our distance from one another,
I twist into a bulbous knot of fabric,
shoved to the back of the drawer.
But once my eyes take sight of yours again,
I unfurl, yanked into the light and shaken free.
The heat of your eyes glide over me
and my wrinkles slowly d i s s i p a t e.

The Smell of your Cologne, Clinging to the Hairs of your Neck

———

Intimately intertwined and sleeping soundly.
The white sheets cushion the crevice of my back.
Unplanned Saturday mornings without a rush to wake.
I roll over and fit my arm through the space under your arm.
My nose finds a home beneath the lazy point of your warm chin
like a hermit crab.

In Your Atmosphere

_____

We rolled on the bed— both blissfully unaware,
surfacing above the blanket the way flying fish do.
Our delirious hearts flapping.
Laughter as contagious as the flu.
Your soul entwined itself with mine
and they laced their transparent fingers.
Our lips caressed while we kissed,
yanking the words from our mouths,
sliding them *down*
                    down
                              down
                                        into our bellies.
Then we dove into bottles of red wine.
We followed each other, swimming to its luscious, ruby depths.
Deeper and darker than what deepness we've known.
Here's to the brilliant ability to be together
for however long—
free as flying fish out of water.

Two-Hour Drives in Traffic

———

Two-hour drives in traffic as
Hondas head home,
and Volkswagens ease slowly into the next lane,
crossing my mind.
Tiptoeing forward,
marching from the back.
Distracting my eyes around
and tapping the beat into the steering wheel.
(bump) (to) (bump)
Anticipating my tongue's bitter bath
of the week's end martini,
and the sting of the tub standing naked
in the crisp October air.
(Pillows)   tossed to the   (side),
          (disregarded) in our (heated) (passions.)
Jealous autumn foliage walks past the car window,
yanking at the side-view mirror,
and sticking its fingers in the spokes of the tires.
It asks about what we'll do,
jerking the car's tailpipe,
trying to slow me down.
I'm not sure.
Friday.
Two-hour drives in traffic.

Our Ceaseless Battles

———

This conflict of emotion:

to be so agonized,
as to be content to never see each other again—
yet at the same instant,
love each other so excessively that
we've forgotten who we are.

An Einstein Dementia

———

He is the answers to every question
I've ever asked myself about life's
reasons when I'm drunk and *s l u r r i n g* and detached
from   myself.
A—balloon—on—a—string.
Him walked up to me, his hand outstretched
in greeting, and soddenly why is an answer.

I don't want anyone speaking to me anymore!
Every new word nudges the sound of his voice further
away and I'm straining to hear it in the past already.
Concerning myself with the sound of spiraling lives
pushes it all from my subconscious.
So I'll be an introvert and reminisce.
You collected the secrets of the galaxy from all the
drawers and shelves and hidden compartments of my
brain and   walked out of   my   universe.
An Einstein dementia.
Please come back and tell me about
the power of a dying star.

Part I: Delicates

———

The washing machine's mouth hangs agape, drooling.
Anxious to taste your scent away.

The risotto cooking in the pan and the dog's breath in the morning
and the stabbing aroma of the mouth wash before bed
and the sea salt body scrub and the peach juice down our chins.

It will chew up your shirt
like a cheap piece of bubblegum,
soak it in saliva,
and spit it back out when the taste disappears
and its jaw starts hurting.

Last time.

A marinated steak smothered in rosemary and a glass of red
wine and coffee at 4am before work and the chlorine from
the pool and the black, sweaty scarves we unwrapped from
our necks after spending the day on the mountain.

Part II: Donation

———

I wish for it.
      My arm
             swimming
through the closet.
How do you fold a life preserver?
      Leaning in,
I wish for it.
My arm
      paddling   desperate
and nearly giving up.
Reaching   far and finding—
I drown
      my face. 'Original Scent'.
      I place it   away
in the bag
and give the pain to someone else
      to wear.

People/ Them

———

Lonely train rides
with no elbow room.
Hand in hand newspapers
tumble beneath the seats,
          having intercourse.
          Intimate.
Eye glances and sideways
stares at the earbuds
blocking it out.
Blocking it all out.
Searching for you
and seeing
other faces and other
people
and things and
people and
emptiness
and nothing.
Do you know him?
Well, shouldn't everybody?
Don't you all?
What happened to—?
three degrees of separation.
Tell him that—.
          Oh, please don't!
Don't forget your belongings.

In Breaths We Babel

———

Speak in tongues of rolling words
unknown or comprehend that come flinging through
the air. Hurling　　　like a spear
　　　　　　　　　　mislead.
Yet how in history could pivot quick
against our flailing ways with words.
Oh, to say a phrase beyond 'hello'!
Hello. Hello. Hello.
Might I confess
and pull you in with words
—to captivate and you to keep.
But must rely on face or charming grin instead.
This burden—oh this heinous pique, of knowing every phrase
for once that I unable say, convey.
Hello! Hello!
What life could different be this all and me if with a
word you flooding speak, may greet my straining ear or
waiting heart to hear.
But nay!
We neither can may say, and must we both then on our way.
Cliché.

Perhaps One Day It Will Be They

How could you know, sweet reader?
For it was only they and me,
easing our pains quietly together just briefly among the many.
You were not there. You were not a part of it.
So why should I give such effort describing,
if you mean to keep roaming these pages for
something you'd understand more directly?
What power are these words against those feelings in that moment?

Oh, but what brilliant magic there was, I tell you!

Perhaps one day it will be they—
holding this book, trying to escape with me again.
And they'll read what I've written about them,
and need not bother with the tediousness of language
because they'll remember,
as I remember.

I'll Keep You Forever Myself

———

I woke up earlier than usual this morning.
You weren't beside me
And I got up quickly, with purpose not to linger in the sheets.
I took my coffee to the porch to breathe
and stood there, listening to the robins start their day.
The red-breasted, motivated, and in lust, and vain robins. Shouting.
Demanding that I teach them your personal melody.
But it's too early and the coffee just burnt my throat.

The Shed

———

Down the stairs of the deck, and the shed at the edge of the grass.
Sunday morning and it's time to mow the lawn.
Yanking the lawnmower free from all the junk in the shed.
The shed watches cars pull into the driveway.
It watches the barbecue,
the group of kids riding their bikes to get ice cream.
The shed sat behind the house and watched our party last month,
wafting humid from the house windows.
Under a sky of summer tinsel is the shed
and us, coming outside to get some fresh air at the edge of the grass.
The air inside the house was turning cotton.
Us and the shed,
watching the party waft humid through the windows.
Then you told me that you loved me
and the shed heard you say it.

Going Out, Going In

Off They Go to Freedom

———

They trek across infinite plains,
seeking refuge and the taste of milk.
Their legs wobble, pushing their weight forward
like they're carrying tubas.
Onward—they beat the Serengeti
beneath their feet. Fleeing from Pharaoh.
The gazelles sprint ahead to paradise
and bring back news of what's to come.
From their noses, stretched to the sky,
we hear brass taps and melodies.
Then the rivers somersault in to baptize
the grassland's crusty forehead.
The waters bring new life.
And on they march for our suffering—
to brood for the world we murder,
rubbing their calloused trunks
over the Earth's carcass in passing.
The elephants pay their respects.
Poachers are coming.
Poachers are always coming.
And we are the poachers, caring.
They must quietly keep moving through the grasses.
What words they'd say otherwise if they could speak a thousand proverbs!
They are quiet and migrating on their pilgrimage
and we must follow them.

Six Brown Sparrows in a Feeder Chirping

―――――

Six brown sparrows are in the feeder, chirping.
Flourishing their robust feathers. Brown.
They chat in a different language.
Immutable words and the secrets to this fleeting life.
They discuss truth brought forth from the heart of the woods,
with aching, frivolous hearts.
Seeds jump from the tray in their excitement.
My eye was on the crimson cardinal—
too introverted to indulge me my questions,
too proud to care, as the sparrows sing so clear.

Startled from my movements,
They   all   take   flight
and I remain grounded in wonder,
waiting for them to come back and tell me more.

Perfection, Infection

————

As I walked through my woods the dying,
I told myself, "I am not magnificent"
—and I knew it.
The screaming crows their words.
Omen, Amen.
Help me find the yellow, sour stones somewhere!
Beneath the crusts of the trees are
only copper ants and moss.
The sun melts overhead.
Cremated to ashes. Rinsed in the ozone strainer.
Sea water tears,,, for the thirsting leaves
that then shrivel up
and die when they gulp it down.
"Take it! I don't need it anymore, soil."
And they drink and they drink.
And they die and they die.
I'll leave my boots near the bank if it matters
and cross into ever-after on the other side,
barefoot.
But all the birds fly backwards (.)

Beyond This Crest, O' Captain

———

And will a whale's spout bellow
secrets of the depths onto the surface of the ocean,
sprinkling recipes for joy across the break of the world,
that only periwinkles be granted access?

The children sing to the snails for their knowledge, if so.
Yet seeing their contorted faces, they close forever.
Ships and their mates will hoardingly net the surf for answers;
then the plovers dive and return less innocent,

in their bills are silvery slivers of hope, to themselves
devoured and savored alone. We've been prevented from the dunes
to ensure a secret's security in the bellies of the birds.
Roll in the sand— the pixie dust of mermaids—

cover yourself in golden powder and kneel before Poseidon.
I'm worthy of your secrets but only admires the shadows
of the everlasting trench. That is where you reside,
and where from the cetacean took its news.

Explore the alluring seas at your will.
To the wondrous walls of Atlantis,
and you will never find reply.
I assure your obsessive mind, unrest.

What Found Among the Fields

———

Encased within a savory skin of ruby,
somehow protected from the harshness of age,
resides the cherry's accustomed soul,
hardened with the reverence of life.

One famished cherry-picker in June
and one cracked molar, thanks to his recklessness.
There must be grace and patience
when eating it, though not for the cherry's sake.

To the Red Country
and part of the gray country of Oklahoma[1]
did spy the fruiting doom upon a stick.
With it grows death and destruction.

Soon the workers leave the orchard,
signaled home by the sound of change in their pockets
and on their backs and in their hands
and everywhere. Forced home in failure.

Placed on the counter is hardly a living.
And placed behind the wheel, driving forever west,
is hardly a man. Buried deep within his pocket
is the cherry from today.

——

Encased within a savory skin of sunlight,
radiating fortune in a liquid of gold,
somehow protected from the hardships of age,
resides the fruit's accustomed soul.

---

[1] Opening line of John Steinbeck's, *The Grapes of Wrath*

This new land brings new food,
and the man finds himself missing his cherries
during the long days in the orchard:
"Them orange juss ain't th' same".

Cries with Skyward Eyes

———

The waxen moon was insatiably envious.
Sycamores reached their burdened limbs to the sky.
The Earth pushes itself further up, the mountains.
Further up the mountains' tears are icicles

covered by the snow and buried deep in a cave.
An ice-picker cannot witness the stars
until he reaches the summit, to peek,
to behold the world, or everything above it.

The beaming sun escapes the winter, barely.
Darkness. Impatience and darkness.
Be the moon granted protection of the skies tonight.
Over time the confidence of the stars grew bright.

As I look at you, you palely look to me.
Boredom drives me home.
A shooting star waves good-bye
though she never caught sight of it.

Yet the eyes stay skyward forever.
And the crystal light of the moon watches the snow.
And the star withers to nothing.
And I make it home just barely alive.

I Am the Woods

———

Needles—
cowering leaves of Sequoias, pulled in with fear—
play me your emerald music.
Whisper into my ear the places you've been and
the sights you've seen, oh babbling brook,
that I might go and see them for   myself.
Let me migrate with birds on
ceaseless journeys   away.
Flying over towns and cities and over forests and mountains,
seeing life pass below me,
following   the moon
and the shades of the   sprinting   sky.
And then I'll brave the emptiness of the open field,
so hushed and sparkling with dew. Quiet as
the downy feathers of a mourning dove, still as mushrooms
clumped together.
The elk raises his majestic head to observe me
approaching, beneath grand, elaborate antlers his body formed.
The pickerel and the perch sew themselves
through currents, stitching the restlessly sleeping river into
blankets of silk to keep the planet warm.
I am the curious owl on the tree branch
and the gray rock rising from the dirt.
I stand at the forest's edge
and feel my spirit within me—the world,
emanating outwards.
It rejoices in the solitude.

For the Female Night

—————

Coy night,
do not hesitate.
There's no reason to be embarrassed or cautious.
Creep across the twilit sky in
purple hues and
bleeding streaks of indigo.
Slowly enter overhead and
show us your star-freckled skin.

Night,
forgive us for such attraction to brightness.
We always greet you backwards,
watching sunsets evaporate, eyes away and looking off.
Oh, how he always swiftly leaves us,
tempted by rebirth, the youth of days to come.
And we pine even more for all things ended,
as we turn to you, cradled in your peppermint breast.

"Oh, but in the Night what life there can be!",
we hear the nightingale proclaim, in his bursts of heart-filled devotion.
And to hear the owl's confession in the cover of darkness,
for you are her friend to whom she speaks so freely.

And Night,
what endurance it takes to listen to your children—
the wolves—
desperately moaning in their canine chorus,
pleading for the warmth of the day's return.
And you must be their humble response!
A mother, understanding.
What might they learn from the impatient and boastful sun,
deaf to their beautiful operas over the noise of his flames?

You give solace to the exhausted moon.
Oh, the pallid love of that fiery sun.
She only reveals herself when she feels safe and protected.
As she does so with *you*.
And to have the tranquility of the world's sweet slumber.
How frantic we are in search of that peace!

Oh Night,
come embrace me with your cooling touch.
Nurse my burns with soft, aloe fingers.
Surround me in those arms and
cover me in your obsidian cloak
that I may gently fall among the pillows

and dream without a worry.

Go Sun, Go!

―――――

Go Sun, Go!
And take our sorrows with you.
Absorb them in your brilliant light, retracting.
Snuff them out with burning heat a-simmer
and bring us joys renewed, tomorrow!

Contemplations on a Park Bench

All the trees are each a galaxy,
pulling stardust up from the soil and
blooming into constellations.
You are the Hubble Telescope,
sitting here on a park bench.
You watch them bend as brachia,
inflating green lungs.
Out There, In Here.
In There, Out Here.
And everything expands.
It's all big and it's all little.
BIG. little. BIG. little—
SPRING. autumn. SPRING. autumn.
Neuron branches grow into
gray matter,
learning the explanations of our
experience. The flora's lovely brains.
Cars pump by through side street veins
and larger highway arteries.
People meander,
passing information about themselves as
hormones, catalysts and ions–molecules motile.
Oh, what lovely nature! What lovely life.
Cells make
tissues
make organs
make organisms make
cultures
make the world
make maker.

The Arrival of this Vernal Youth

———

Spring is a young man,
emblazoned—
with the stench of the sun wafting off him.
He leaps out, arrogant and boastful,
and catches us off guard.
I can feel his hot breath
coming in off the ocean—
a guttural war-cry, announcing winter's defeat.
We relish in his adolescent frolics, basking in his rudeness.

Alone-Together;

Or, Sapiens

We Murder Dandelions

———

We murder the innocent dandelions,
casually blowing their heads off
      with a privileged wish.
Their gray hair is
        shaved, and   swims
across
the   field
      like tiny, schooling   minnows
fleeing   oppression . .   . .

The wind will try to save the
weeds,

pulling them   away from the
extent of our hands, in loud, airy protests.

We are entitled and unwilling to reach farther,
so we don't.

The clouds do nothing,
     floating by overhead
     and the wind keeps p u l l i n g
     the dandelions and calls us bigots,
rushing by our ears, yelling for help.

Lunchtime

―――――

At lunchtime, I walked through the park.
The pile of papers on my desk is thirteen stories high.
And I was scolded by my boss when I was late to an important meeting.

For fifteen minutes, I sauntered my way around,
watching the squirrels hopping on the grass.
Children were playing tag as their mothers looked on from the corner of
their eyes.
A young couple read together on a blanket with their shoes off,
though the book wasn't interesting them much.

I took a seat under the shade of a tree,
my back against its knotty trunk, and closed my eyes.
The sounds of the people around me in the park
kept my interest, and I listened,
taking a rest on a clear summer day. Simple. Stress Free.

I opened my eyes again, blinded momentarily by the sunlight,
and glanced at my watch.
Lunchtime had ended twenty minutes ago.

Unconventional Dream

[from magazine clippings]

———

People ask chromosomes the simplest sort of opinions,
of the soul, of this country—to figure out our undeniable obsession with
brilliance.
We really just wanted the reflexes of being separated to shoot the
unrelenting pressure of what we are not.
Depressed and unmotivated, I decided to keep His dreams alive.
The promise to remain fair dove head first and landed in
a factory for the untouchable world.
Time for a drastic change.

The City of My Surrender;

or, Boston, Massachusetts

———

Ivy climbs up the brownstones' sunburnt faces.
Cobbled back allies where secluded lamps are head bent and brooding.
Stairwells lead to the powdered aroma of bread, fresh from the oven.
The sizzle of cigars, fiery and fierce between fingers.
Businessmen loosen their ties before each ordering a Negroni.
An arrogant smell of chocolate in the next room
fits itself beneath the door to join the commotion.
Beaches in November, wrapping their arms around the bay to keep it warm,
hushing the dunes that are nesting.
Espresso martinis leave rings of water on the table.
Oriental rugs chuff beneath the soles of your shoes.
The Buddhist hum of the neon lights in Chinatown.
Cars rush along the river. Sailboats slice like butter knives.
Fragments of solitude in the shadow of chaos.
Museums and their sleeping sculptures. The paintings take extended naps.
Nighttime, and looping into restaurants and bars. Speak easy.
Just around the next corner, bumping into tales of the past.
Young, millennial skyscrapers glare at you with a hundred, splendid eyes.
Their grandmother-houses are hunched behind them,
creaking and arthritic.
Purple balls of Allium. And baseball in the park, come spring.
Ducks trumpet at one another, bouncing brass voices across the water.
The royal swans march in unison.
Below the pavement rises a piercing metal screech:
the soprano whistle of the subway.
Incessant commuters. Incessant horns.
People rushing as salmon in migration,
shouldering their way up to the mountains of New Hampshire
and Vermont on the weekend.
Highways, platforms, escalators, stairs.
Small doors in smaller crevices.

Ebbing droplets of people. Oil in water.
7am into the city. 7pm out of the city.
Continued escapes toward the forested retreats of suburban silence.
Neighborhoods that rest on the puckered lips of rural hilltops,
with views of the city's shining eyes, looking up into the stars.

Pudgy

———

He broods in the corner of a party,
accompanied by a caramel scotch.
Bitter both.
We move about the patriarch as planets turning freely,
waiting for the sun to *POP!*
He tells the cup a secret—
lips to its ear and whispering a sip.
The birds eventually return for spring
and fly through his chest,
fanning at the long-since-burning embers.
The scotch crackles within him.
Blooming orange renegade.
One second he's a recluse,
the next he's subtle fanfares.
Stretching like a peacock,
transforming folds in origami.
Turning orange.

Finally.

Passenger Emergency

―――

(an experiment with trains)

Mild Alzheimer's. *Unsaid.*
Sharing your wishes.
Create.
Share.
For not more than 10 days.
Emergency.
Lean against, through your own priority
and personal stories.
Get started
on the people you love.
Forward.
Something controlled and monitored.
In case of emergency,
press button to speak
directly to train operator.

The Woman Winsor

———

An Ode to Queen Elizabeth II

Oh to be a thin, gold chain on the wrist of royalty.
A living figure of history yet to come,
radiating the collapse of nations and the birth of kingdoms,
sitting quaint and composed on a simple, grey chair.
Fathers and Mothers and Grandfathers forever before and forever after.
The past inherited, coronated, and passed down to the next.

Oh to be a small broach upon the determined chest of a Queen
and her white pearls around her neck.
Behind closed doors run grandchildren down carpeted hallways and
through gold-encrusted guest rooms.
Small, plump corgis waddle at her ankles.
They would gladly lick her face if given a chance,
and would not feel an ounce of disrespect.

Her contagious chuckle of joy requests the presence of my own.
Her Majesty smiles good morning to the nervous maid,
having noted the faint shake of the girl's leg when she curtsied yesterday.
Now to sit at her desk to assess the world and its orders.
She fingers the thin, gold chain in thought,
trying to convey her very human feeling.

Miss

———

The woman crouches to help the little
girl to her feet, brushing
the dirt from her knee and
society's views from her eyelashes.
She tends to the children
and eventually calls them back
to the classroom.
A mother duck.
She will teach them more about
this corrupt, albeit beautiful, deceitful world.

Lessons in American History

———

Do you see my cowering face and bloodied back?
You're viewing us through the eye piece.
Exits are towards the rear.
It will be four years next month.
Aluminum cans crushed by panic.
Bullets lay smoking, taking my last breath for me.
Contorted gasps drowned out in panic
amid the cataclysmic chaos of Paradise
that we must bid adieu.
Lights.
Red, yellow, blue, green.
Light.
White.
His face is pressed into the grass.
Her hair clings to the pavement,
crawling away, pulling at her lifeless scalp.
Do you see my cowering face and bloodied back?
Are you seeing?

Enough.

Pulse

———

You do not have an identity to me,
assassin(.)
You snuffer of existence.
You nameless ~~being~~ thing,
observing the progress of
America
and terminating it of your own accord—...
Starting over?
If possible(.)
assassins are all the same.
As Death through moving
history. There. And There.
Bang. And Bang.
Hovering overhead and landing
abruptly in your chest.
Four letters is brief enough.
But to strip it more
and leave them lifeless(.)
Have I done your will?
And succeeded absolutely.
Aiming and beating
the quo of this country into even more panic.
Is anyone there?

As My Own

———

Reach out your trembling hand to
me, dear brother.
For mine has been stretched in yearning too,
finding nothing but self-hatred and despair.
Give me your hand, my friend,
that we might save one another.
Our waves strike
the same length of land,
swelling from the vast oceans
of our puddle hearts.
I am here— and sooner die than betray.
Lean your head on my shoulder, sweet brother.
Let me absolve your doubts
and show you true comfort.
We, as troubled souls
inconspicuous.
Give me your sorrow, my friend,
that I may take it as my own.
For what happens to you quickly raptures my heart
in pain.

Apple

———

Insanity: losing your grip on the world!
Me. Us. Them. I. Together?
Volcanoes, digging down.
Death from the mouth, spitting black.
Cancer ridden trees and smoke.
Flaming water, burning coasts.
Rainbow warriors raging.
Me. Us. Them. I.

The Saxophone Player Outside the Hospital

He leans back,
tipping the music onto his face, bathing in it,
cleansing himself of his pains.
His eyes are closed—
comprehending otherwise.
The two of them sway,
dancing in the street.
Everything is wet and twinkling.
Tears are thrown from car windows speeding past.
     It's all too   swift
to appreciate such handsome melody.
He and his instrument
forever shout the pains and loss
into the ignorant, cynical city
to whomever will stop and listen.
To you! To me!
A hoarse metal voice sings us all
to sleep and carries the weary-hearted.
We are still foolish,
but oh so beautiful.

I Found my Muse in the Ocean

I found my muse in the ocean.
A goddess, whom I forever desired.
She was standing in the water, as I looked at her from the sand.
The water groped her thighs, hinting at the space between her legs.
She was curvy and voluptuous.
Hair like honey.
The white cloth was all she had to shield her from our mortal eyes.
But it was wet and transparent. It draped on her like a jellyfish.
Waves yanked at the fabric, trying to strip her naked.
She handed me a pomegranate, before finally being taken by the sea.

All the Good Ones

———

Onward to the Red Orchard!, he cursed.
He ate soup with a fork,
scribbling the rules of the game into a notebook—
undecipherable.
In thought we gibberish, code for chaos, his of the mind was continual.
Murmurs we could not hear because we never listened to his rambling
mouth,
behind
cigarette smoke and
between
foul words.
Fast kisses to the cheek.
Do we read random notes about nothing?
Chuckling at obscurities sparked from the barrel of a gun.
A genius in psychosis.
Only I know the eagles are owls.

Nobel Prize

———

What bravery!

They did not know
how to even tie their own shoes once.
But now?
Now, they are studying
biochemistry and integral calculus and
topics only savants can master.
Bracing their intellect to outwit
the ways of life and
the instructions outlined by our DNA
to beget corruption and faults in gene editing.
Here they are, these challengers,
in squat, glass, science buildings
following the silent voice of
God within them,
working through them and
guiding them to answers yet discovered.
They focus in on the tiniest of cells in
little
plastic
dishes
under
microscopes,
seeing through the eyes of the Creator,
experimenting.
They examine a single letter of this book of life
in writing and suggest a correction.

In their hands they hold a stone.

Change

———

From 1923—
sipping on champagne,
shivering in the glass like maracas.
This was the Jazz Age.
And you bump through the party,
through the guests all laughing like champagne
in the glass.
Everyone is smiling and ignorant.

To 1968—
a more morose and brooding decade
when the cherry blossoms wilted before growing.
This time we're pushing against glass-plated
shields and throwing our eyebrows down into
the projects of our forehead, yelling at them to stay there.
Everyone is screaming and learned.

Then into the new millennium of a truly
enigmatic system of society.
Pulling the brain tissue from our skulls and
stuffing it into bank accounts.
Destroying ourselves to have nothing accepted.
Taking train rides here while across the ocean
there, in Singapore, Swaziland or Tokyo.
Oblivious to corruption, since 1923.
Murdering dreams, since 1968.

One hundred years like that, and back again!
Now I understand the loop of infinity.

And then

Succession's Kin

———

He rubs his woman's pumpkin hip,
pulling her close to his side and
searches for peace
and reassurance from his vengeful, hateful anger.
Both of his children are okay, thank God.
Surviving
through indifference
and frustration the same,
amid hostility
and corruption elsewhere, everywhere.
Relieved and now release to
low tide sighing.
She scrapes the dough, caked onto the counter.
The table skin—removing melanin.

Subjective

———

The days are s   l   o   w,
The weeks are fast,
The months are s l   o   w,
The years are fast,
The decades are s l   o   w,
The lifetime is fast.
Stretching out for your entire existence,
sitting on a nucleus(.)

A Dedication to Sunday Dinners at The House

———

My Father to the right.
The closest comparison I have to Jesus
Christ, with all his loyalty, forgiveness,
and unyielding Love.

My Mother across.
Her strength brought me into this world,
and she continually strengthens my hope
in humanity by her commitment to care
for others.

My Sisters on the left,
for whom I would gladly surrender every
wish I've ever had for a brother if it meant
keeping them for myself.

Bare-knuckled Fighters

———

You prize-fighters!,
swinging those calloused fists within the ring.
For what do you fight and brave against more perils?
For Love?
Is it for your steadfast morals of that flaming heart?
Is it for the waving lands of this beautiful country?
Fight on! For we are here,
pressing ourselves against your back.

—

What strength!
The rippling form of their large, round shoulders
thrusting forth the arm.
Do you see the camaraderie of the body
and the effort of it all?
How the muscles work with the tendons
and how the tendons work with the frame.
The eyes, the heart, the neurons.
What honor there lies in fighting for what you value.

Pairs Of

———

I sit and watch happiness.
The children run out of their sneakers,
greeting their grandmother.
Green stains climb up the legs of their pants.
And pairs of hands, gliding over handrails
and pulling bills from wallets, and coins from pockets,
passing money to cashiers.
The men shake hands.
He smiles at her.
Hands clasping—
Thumb to thumb to
pointer to pointer to
middle to middle to
ring beside metallic ring beside
two caressing pinkies, reaching around.

I sit and observe contentment.
Questions have answers and I have me.
How have you been?
Morning reaches for Night's hand,
guiding her onto the dancefloor from the East.
Spring wakes Winter from his slumber
with a violet kiss gently to his cheek.
Eyes, scanning. Two opaque films of keratin watching.
He reaches his arm around her shoulder.
She eases her weary cheek into the hill of his chest,
sighing contently.
I am waiting.

Hearing Those Whispers

___

Whispers
[to change your ways and make you question—]
But this is you in perfection,
                    and this is
life

in disregard.

To Walter, To William and to Sweet Marguerite

———

1

I will sing my song, forever, unwavering—
shoving penny whispers between the
couch cushions when my mother's
attention goes elsewhere.
I'll toss some loose words into his clanking
cup and slyly leave a few sentences tucked
gently into the check, *Thank you very
much.*
And to myself I'll guard my spot. *No you
don't! Back up!* Because, Me!, unmarked
or mutilated. *Read it again. Read it again.*
For the word is truth. And the word
is God.
*You know, baby, you just might be the most
magnificent woman I've ever met in my
entire life.* Sunlight through the slats.
Masks unworn and cast aside.

II

Here I am beside you, comrade.
I place my hand on your strong, inhaling
chest that you may know my anthem.
I feel my gusty spirit billowing within you.
My hands are your hands. My hands
are the tree's hands. I have the same
eyes as the skyscraper—reflecting and
clear. What compounds and atoms and
biology cling to my bones rightfully cling
to yours. Then let's be connected
to this and to that. Let's feel the silk
between it all.
Acknowledge the breath within your-self
and seeing your coffee's breath steaming
from the cup on the table. The mountain
and the sun's breath, radiant, expelling
out over the mountain out there in front
of you.
This is where we are and this is where
you've taught me to be,

in pieces—separate but together.

III

Oh, to be constantly nudged by the
lustful soul.
To feel the sharp stabs of the arrow and
the pen
as I place it against my notebook.

I'm surrounded by words—yours—
and yearn to add my own.

You speak through time and what you
say lands
gently on the valleys of my ear, gliding
down into
its tunnels. Your masterpieces clog the
deltas of
my heart, rising from the throat.

Writing as fast as you can to trap the
sensation of
life. Pinning it to the page.

Using your pen-scythe to slash at
preconceptions—
surrendering to the vastness of the
world and
pushing the shape of it through the
bleeding end,
lubricated by ink

IV

Dropping petals, dispensing work—
as nothing is
solitary,

I know. For
the spirit of God is made up of WE.
Each of us alive in the other and I will
permit you to live on within me if I
myself in you.

This I promise surely.
And thus is my poem.
And thus is myself.
And thus as we are, in the hopes of
ever being.

Clamming

———

She wades through an estuary at low tide.
The slop of her muffled boots—pulling.
Muscular thighs, freckled with brown mud, keep stepping
and the trees sway together.
Plodding.
She is not bothered but carries on walking in search of some clams
and does not get stuck.

The Baggage Claim at the Airport

———

A self-conscious baggage claim,
spinning anxious.
Chiding thoughts internal.
A Louis Vuitton bag,
and banging paranoia.
"There it is."
Here's a piece of
what I used to carry.
Taken away by whomever.
Alone and spinning in self-doubt.
Up comes another bag,
rising from inside,
presented to be taken.
The girls giggle as they walk away.
And eventually all the bags are gone.

And I Must Face Uncertainty

————

We brush against lifetimes on the dancefloor, moving to the music,
dancing with their eyes closed.
Our shirts tug at each other as we walk through everyone.
They sense something we aren't able to.
Tipsy at the bar and
they ask for what you want.
We pass them on the street or
sitting on the subway.
                    Lives in living lives.
One form of your future
exits   out   the   door just now
and departs from the presence of your eyes
to join the masses. And you had no idea.
A small streak brushed onto the ever-painted canvas,
disappearing into the collage.
Gone forever
but took revolving doors and still unknown.
Abracadabra.
I glance up from reading on the train to
rest my eyes between chapters,
and seeing you, I ask myself:
Are we partners in the future?
Will I get to know your friends and the
impressions you place on them?
Will it be this shoulder you utilize one day in all your aching hardships?
Perhaps, but now we are strangers.
I thank you for holding the door and for
my three beautiful children.
Fourth dimension r e a c h e s.
"Thank you."
"You're welcome."

Here We Are, Here I Am

———

What, is, life, but, an, infinite, amount, of, commas.
Pauses, and, breaths.
Suspense,
Waiting,
Fear,
Anxiety,
before, pressing, on, and, moving, into, the, next, moment, unsure, of, the,
Unknown, but, staying, and, going.
And, the, importance, of, placement.
Where, to, place, yourself, in, this, life.
A, rule.
A, guideline, sometimes, hardly, followed.
Hardly, a, rule, at, all.

Go and Ask a Black Man

———

Go and ask a Black man
what privilege you can strip him of.
Let him convey the sheer freedom of chains
and systemic discrimination
against the backdrop of genocide and Caucasian agendas.
His hands are bound, but they are black and they are clean—

Go and ask a Black man
how he watched the master beat the wife
and the innocent spirit of America and
how he was beaten for the sake of his own,
to give her everything he could amidst the oppression
and death.

Go and ask a Black man
how he identifies his color.
Why in the blackness of ya' eyes an'
in the blackness of ya' weapons, suh.
That's right, ya' filth.
And ask him where her road will end.

Go and ask a Black man
to stand out there, exposed,
with his eyes shackled shut.

Go and ask a Black man
how to make him kneel in protest and
how to force him to his feet once more.

Go and ask a Black man
how much pigment crisps his skin.
Or, better yet, take it without asking first,
like they did to Henrietta,

and like they did to MLK,
and like they did to Oscar Grant,
and like they did to Trayvon Martin,
and like they do to all the rest.

Go and ask a Black man
how to manage endless hope
when all we do is
confine and restrict and deprave him,
in lasting pressures to conform.

Jack Dunbar

Maternal Instinct

Her innate sense of motherhood is
a recessive gene.
Slapped onto a milk carton.
Pulling objects, pushing people.
She forgets who you are,
but remembers to cause you pain from the beginning.
Spirit contortions and masquerades.
Having the will but not the power to
protect either one.
Alone— with you— thank God.
Undeserved daughters,
affirmed in ways unorthodox.
And you care.
And you care.
And you care.

Ernest

[changed from 'Addictions']

———

You tell me yours and
I'll tell you mine—
But let's remember that we're
just men
and that the pressures of living,
mixed with the stress of surviving,
make us do things we wouldn't otherwise
want to.

Tenders

———

Frisky bartenders,
throw
fingers in the air.
They juggle martini glasses,
spin bottles,
make immaculate cocktails with silver thimbles.
Chemists,
keeping up with the pace of their orders.
While people in queues,
outside along the sidewalk,
are held together by swan neck stanchions.
Skittish herds of sheep pressed by velvet rope.

It Was Good

Turning in the Horses

―――――

He grips tightly to the cold, leather reigns
and leads the weary horses into their stalls for the night.
Their hooves snowplow the aroma of fresh aspen bedding into the air.
The barn is stagnant and warm.
At the sound of oats filling their bowls,
their ears rotate forward. Bulrush around the pond.
On their necks he places a chilled, calloused hand
and smiles into their observant eyes, snapping his tongue to keep them calm.
Then he cleans them with a brush that shushes them all quiet,
crouching to remove dried mud from around their ankles while they eat.
Before turning off the light, he drapes wool blankets over their backs.
Their suede hips are swaying contently, and they sigh,
warmed after a bitter day in the corrals outside.

Bikes Against the Fence

———

The bikes are against the fence.
Around their necks are large chains
and bike locks keeping them in a choke hold.
Silver strands of floss between
the fence's teeth, clenching their throats.
I can hear them calling me to set them free when I walk by.
Their tires are rubbed bare.
The seats sag like furrowed eyebrows, pleading.
They are ridden here every morning
and do so gladly
if it means feeling the wind rush past them.
They spread their handlebar-arms wide.
The pedals turning and the gears changing is
a chuckle of delight,
until they're home and locked up again,
where they wait for the next moment of utter bliss.

S'mores Around the Fire in Summertime

———

A fatal caress of the flame.
A moment—
just long enough for the marshmallow
to bare the heat of the fire
before giving up and burning.

SAW/WAS

———

Reflections// on everything.
Store front windows downtown.
Standing in the water
on an August day,
legs submerged.
Crowded parties
and closing the bathroom door. *Click.*
On your own—
away from the sounds
to assess your own form
and figure.
Your eyes are red with drunkenness.
Your mind is red with life.
Spoons in your hand during breakfast.
Seeing who we are.
Seeing ourselves in the reflections
and seeing everything in the reflections.
Both—
Disgusted and intrigued.

Pancake

———

Listen to the music of your voice. Melodic.
Hear the syllables and the sounds of 's' as it wrestles with
your teeth.
Your tongue is a flounder pulled in by the fisherman,
flapping on the boat.
It slaps like a steak on the grill, sizzling,
lubricated by your spit, lathered in barbeque sauce.
And the aggressive sound of 'k' in the word *pancake*,
throwing a punch into the air, trying to hit you in the face.
Cake.
Cake.
Your palate-guard holding back your breath.
The bouncer checking IDs.
Go ahead,
then pushing forward like a splinter.
Cake.
Cake.
Appreciate the symphony in the movement of your lips and
the cadence of your diction,
knowing the power of phrase—
words and their beautiful music,
going out forever
and never coming back.

Two Ice Cubes Floating in a Cup

———

Two   (ice) (cubes)   floating in a cup.
They dip, they rise, they bounce and pirouette around each
other in twirls each time I move.
If I turn too quickly, they trip and knock into themselves.
One catches the other and lifts it to its feet.
One Two Three, One Two Three.
The ice cubes slowly rotate in their dance.
Genderless and in love and dancing
in a world all their own,
shrinking from the heat of their affections.

The Jacket Hanging Beside the Door

―――――

The jacket beside the door
collapses, exhausted, into the coat rack's arm.
It wafts the stench of hard labor
that started at 4 o'clock in the morning,
when fresh bales of Timothy hay were delivered.
I heard the metal knocker on the door jingle when he came in
and listened to his groans when he slid the jacket off his shoulders.
It's trying to catch its breath before tomorrow
when the work will begin again, bright and early.
The shed needs to be repainted and
the wooden fence has a few broken posts to be replaced.
The thick, chestnut hide is soaking wet,
darkened by the torrential rainstorms that haven't stopped in days.
Water drips to the floor and clops against the ceramic tiles like sweat.

Beach Day

———

He reaches a tan, sandy hand to the back of his
neck and grips the collar of his shirt.
Its knees go weak and it crumples in his grip.
Finally touched and swooning.
In one swift motion, his arm extends, and the
fabric peels off him, pulling up like a
theatre curtain.
It slides a cotton palm up his
creamy, fondant back
and swan dives over his lush head of hair,
inhaling the shampoo he massaged into his
scalp this morning while he showered,
naked.

Laying and Lying

Faggot

———

It's not difficult being a faggot.
All you must do is exist against the word of
God, the creator of all things.
And disobey the laws of human nature and biology.
And be an abomination.
And be a repulsed, foreign species among humanity
and be something different that genetics can't explain.
It's simply being yourself.

It's not difficult being a faggot.
All with a meager kiss that sodomizes the human
condition to create life naturally,
the way God intended.
And years and years and years of self-hatred.
Sorting through emotions,
balancing self-love and self-disgust, while you have
affairs that make you feel alive and human for once.
Accepting exile in both places.
Walking through the valley of death.
Do you remember how quickly you shoved
him into your pocket so no one would catch you?
In manhunt, you must keep quiet.

It's not difficult being a faggot.
And saying: I'm sorry I'm not who you've imagined—
to your family, to your friends, and to someone else.
But also, I'm not sorry for who I am
but mainly I'm so sorry. Please forgive me.
We'll have to adapt and adopt
to fit our altered form of fatherhood, but that's okay.
They won't be ours for real,
but they'll love us just the same.

It's not difficult being a faggot.
Or being the last one chosen—
The boys' elbows and the boys'
       exclusion
and the boys, making me dribble
to see how I do it so differently.
They know something I'm not
aware of yet.
I'm sure it doesn't affect
my young, developing purpose
to belong on the team or
within my own body.
It's fine.
I'm growing up.
I'm learning how to
com-part-mental-ize and lie.

It's not difficult being a faggot.
It's not.
It's not difficult.
It's not.

Ms. Madison Vinton

———

Sitting in front of the mirror backstage,
He becomes *She.*
Light bulbs framing the vanity, watch her
transformation and glow with pride.
She can hear the bar getting louder out there.
Business is good. They come to see her.
Allies and family congeal around the stage with
wads of one-dollar bills in their hands.

"You're on in three, honey."
Now for the finishing touches.
Lipstick. Mascara. Perfect.
Hidden and ever visible
beneath a fabulous wig.

She takes one final look at her momma's photo,
pinched between the glass and the wood of the vanity,
as she does every night before she performs.
"I love you, Momma. This is for you, always."

Heels on the floor
as her introduction begins.
The crowd goes wild.

A Brief Intimacy with Shame

———

Before:
checking over my shoulder.
Quickly!
People in crowds with glock fingers.
Glancing.
Pointing.
Red hand blinking. STOP!
The three-headed traffic light.

Before:
sweaty palms.
And two women
cooing like white mourning doves.
Hearing crows planning murder.
Looking at the finger.
Looking at the hands, together.
Paralyzing fear and
letting go.

Here We Are Safe

———

Our bed is our fortress.
The sheets are running barricades, stretching around the perimeter.
The pillows are soldiers resting,
slumped white in liberating surrender.
Come and lay beside me in our acropolis.
Come escape the hardships
of this horrible, bitter, exhausting life.
Let's tangle ourselves in the duvet
where I can kiss you frantically
without fear.
I must head off for war soon,
where we cannot ask and
where we cannot tell—
so kiss me now while we're here.
Kiss me while you can.

Let Me Do It On My Own

———

I've been clutching this grenade all eternity.
And I've pulled the pin too late.
Do not try to save me now,
or else us both engulfing.
Remember those wonderful memories?
My fingers are raw and bleeding
from holding icy flashbacks.
What would you like me to tell you
and how does it make me feel?
Horrible—
Rejected—
Lifeless—
I know
the tissue box is empty.
What should I do with these ticking
heart beats
and the grenade in my hand?
Tell me, so that I can survive this or
am I to fend for myself?

Lonny

———

Sprout from crescent water, Daisy.
Duel that fearsome beast in belt!
Pain becomes **Pleasur.**
Depleting *Pleasure* becomes **Pain.**
Haven't you figured that
Hurting/*Healed.*
Dream/**Reality.**
Memory/**Experience.**
Love/**Hate**//
[**Love.**]
Let's revert to youth forever
so we can be young boys again.
We'll witness and relate
in colored hues, flashing emerald on the water,
growing.
You and I, or He and You and I between,
/controlled. /
Living Little Lives.
LO. *LA.*

Fruit Boy

―――

Little nervous fruit boy, with all your gentle sweetness pouring.
Oh how the supple skin goes blooming bashful— love inspired.
Formed within the sunlight of acceptance peace. Delayed.
Might in turning gold from kindness swell that caring world
you've needed now and then forever, always.
Let me see that sweetest face in all your blemished glory,
you little smiling fruit boy.
And plant a healing kiss right here
that all your worries flee henceforth.

What are all these constant troubles, little nervous fruit boy?
Why are you despondent?
Shame begets sin—the pity-pain within.
Oh don't go closing off,
you little aching fruit boy.
Stay awhile, so we might see that lovely nature
come alive and save us all—as much as you,
my perfect little fruit boy.

You Do Not Want My Blood

———

The hospital beds all have a body in them.
Nurses leave at the end of their shifts, out of breath and
debilitated, ready to crawl into bed and die of exhaustion.
Blood reservations are depleting quickly.
Go away, none of that is good here!
We don't accept that health insurance.
Family members only.
And surgeons sweat faster—
missing loops in the suture.
I'll get to the point(.)
we'd rather swine as saviors.

Sentence

———

I couldn't wrangle the words back any longer.
As tightly as I pulled the statement's leash,
the animal was still more powerful, and it overtook me.
There are deep callouses plastered over the roots of my fingers now
and it's out.
It's over.
It's done.
It's alive,
        careening through everything.

Rampant.

We Are the Purple Lilacs

––––––

We are the purple lilacs
whose bones stand naked and shivering
outside the window most of the year.
We are those lilacs that finally burst in summer—
convincing everyone for two brief weeks
how beautiful we truly are.
Their purple elbows slump over the picket fence
and butterflies have affairs with each plume.
You can smell the purple lilacs driving around town.
Then one day the lilacs wilt and they die,
just as everything starts really blooming.
Everyone is sad and tuts but quickly forgets—
until we bloom next year
and the car windows are rolled down again.
We are the purple lilacs.

Sonnets

Sonnet 5

How quick the thought intrudes our mind's display.
Suggests a fault in form that holds an err.
We brush aside the constant fears. Away!
Yet feels the doubt— cannot equate. Don't bear
supposed mistakes! They breed more fear— a front.
All eyes' regard these sheening spots reflect,
that bouncing back ourselves we must confront.
Such modeled sights come drilling in— affect.
And then we change the way we've been create
to better fit this altered form anew.
We saw the bone, impact the lip. Inflate
the breasts become. Our forehead skin so few
      the wrinkled lines, decrease and disappear.
      The mold we show the world is insincere.

Sonnet 9

To be revealed a wondrous thing of friends,
that I have neither known nor have. Regret
to dedicate a freely hand that mends
his heart's distraught. It's trust. One mustn't fret.
And "Lo!", I'll cry, when like the frigid rain,
upon this glistened glass as streaming here,
does flowing eyes become. So rapt' in pain.
They're drenched beyond repair think I. So queer!
I take along the hardened ache, divine.
In time shall shed and will begin again.
And all I'll do is all I've known: confine.
One day they'll come and all the brothers, men.
      Remain a friend and all your love to give
      companions them, to in those moments live.

Sonnet 11

Behold! I find myself in artwork shown.
And recognize the marbled shape to be
myself as cast a mastered, molded stone.
Existence carved to life organically—
Of me, in history. Before that came
this day, does spilling forth from jeroboams?
Plus, how can we deny that we the same
all be as endless epics, rhyming poems,
those portraits on the wall? In frame,
portray us back in rich artistic feats.
So pass through filled museums that may proclaim
humanity, to understand. Completes
    the mystery of life and what proposed
    by artful themes as these, with you transposed.

Sonnet 13

When all my atoms formed and came to groups
within my mother's womb, the genes had locked
and zipped in strands unlike *these* males. Through hoops
I, growing, leapt and birthed a boy that mocked
how so the way should be had been us made.
I screaming cried and had my toes and hands,
though in my cells a brewing change was laid.
It broke the mold as people them demands.
When one day fast, a young, sweet boy become
to running by the sterner boys he skipped.
I smelled the plants. I cared much harder from
this frolic heart than all of them. As script
      my ways the genes have done to make me as
      this happy soul you see with such pizazz.

Sonnet 16

Your eyes have jinxed my heart amused in sight.
My legs you left to hold my flustered state.
For I should be compared, to face this plight?
True beauty drives all those at such a rate!
And when you say your words my mind will melt.
Like as you wink, my gut would move about.
Wordléss will sum of which to have been dealt.
But love deceives, as you may too, no doubt.
My heart cannot withstand much more. Oh can't
I know for sure that love will just exist
because of this and all my hopeless rant?
I may regret, but always will persist.
  Forgive us both, and on my heart no blame.
  I leave to you the choice to stoke this flame.

Sonnet 25

Of all the life you've given me in heart,
must I so reckless go from this, and purge?
So what of all the hurt? Might rapid part,
or bare, haphazard comprehend? Emerge—
Through lens will harder I examine truth
of each requirement of passion's spark.
Then slowly start to trust again as proof
to my unfailing soul may reembark.
Yet once again begin to recreate,
with even all the halting fears remain.
Like swelling sea does rising up, inflate,
to on the tightened sand may crash again.
   And hoping that with time might loosen more
   the hard-packed grains of stretching beach ashore.

Sonnet 50

My sweet Selena dear, the night forbid
your frosted face before my golden glare.
Hyperion has cast my look as did
to thee. Oh ravage me into despair
and strip this raging light away for good!
Please blot me out from in the sky. Erase,
to not exist, or be misunderstood.
A simple snuff of ailments burned through grace.
As whence began has been us both in view
of each one else, but us. And Erebus
continues thus! But in your phasings flew
may coupled over Earth monogamous.
       Thereby the planet peace we spinning be,
       so all our days as one can guarantee.

Sonnet 52

Have I sat here to watch the going sun
withdraw, to hide below the wood, come eve'?
Will in himself be calm to set? To dun—
Tis' he controls the time until the lay.
Yet nay decides to part from Earth today.
To pence the change, and always have the morn'.
All pined—the forest bright by dulling ray,
and even passed the ho'r. "For night's not here."
Might ease his heart, in bitterness forlorn.
Could doff this chariot would he. Austere.
And stay with us, in fearing blackness born,
some raptured sky to darkness come tonight.

     In seeing anxious ways, that needn't scorn,
     will pray by midday light, in thanking, sight.

K. 03

I hear it— in the world around me, here.
Majestic songs of life that will compose—
It's beating symphony of drums, so near
the hearing chimmings roll. A crashing pound,
the cymbal break. An iridescent sound
that cradles such a youngling spirit grow.
My ears reject the want to turn, they're bound.
Sweet symphony of notes, we stretch from you!
And grow the world had done indeed. I know
the great conductor of this song, renew!
Cast up the band and make these teachings show.
Give chills to even winter's wind— and keep
the wondrous song a-play, and let it flow.
       And on we go and on we ever go.
       For all this world you hope, and listens hear.

Prose

All They Found was Treasure

———

Cape Cod curled her finger and coaxed the greedy eyes of European men across the sea—beckoning them. But she wasn't trying to give them anything. She was trying to correct their mistakes, like a mother does for her ignoble children. She was talking from the mouths of the Native Americans but these new people could not understand the strange dialect.

Not that they were listening.

Impatient, they quickly decided the truth in the matter. They were industrialized and learned. What could these savages know?

There was no mistaking the finger wanted to reward them, when they looked through their telescopes and from under the brims of their hats. Her words were ignored and they looked past her, confident in what she was showing them.

They could see all the gold behind her, glimmering softly on the shores. "We must go to these new lands," they cheered, shaking with anticipation, imagining the wondrous discoveries they could make. They packed their weapons and off they went, venturing to this new world to be the first ones there.

But when they arrived, the gold wasn't gold at all—It was just sand, relaxing next to the ocean, sunbathing. Their ships had made it, and they were alive, but they did not care. The men knelt, grabbing large fistfuls of sand that quickly escaped through their fingers, while they yelled and cried to their god overhead.

They kept searching and found yellow ears of corn growing peacefully from the elbow of giant green leaves, cradling them. They rallied together and cut down all the crops.

The aliens sweat beneath the radiant sun, who had finally been unmasked, showing his face. His light reflected off the leathery backs of

Rainbow Trout slipping beneath the palm of the river. One by one all the fish were caught and seared on the open fire. A "celebration".

From the trees came all forms of life.

But these people wanted more, and they destroyed everything trying to find it.

In Love with Hiccups

I was talking with someone about something. (I can't remember all those useless details). I was holding a plastic cup in my hand. *Bud light* was written on the cup in large blue letters. The bar was loud and distracting. People shouted about random, unimportant things: *What song is this? How are you? Can I get you a drink? Have you talked to someone about it?*

I'm not sure what I was talking about, but then your energy entered the conversation and I lost whatever thought held me to the earth. You casually listened to me speak, standing there, harmless. Your eyes were being fanned by large palm leaf eyelashes and a gold chain ran its finger down your buttery neck, and your shoelaces. *Chris, I want you to cut your hair like this.*

Either the beer was finally dulling my senses or your soul was leaning into mine. I had to keep myself steady. Maybe I was too drunk. Maybe I shouldn't drive later. Maybe I was in love with you this quickly.

You randomly introduced yourself in the middle of her talking to make sure I knew your name because to know a person's name is to know everything about them.

My lustful eyes, insatiate and craving more, bounced to you incessantly after that like a tennis ball. I look at you, you look at me, I look at you, you look at me. For a moment I thought our eyes held longer than normal. Maybe you were just being a good listener and looking back at someone when they look at you. But there you are looking at me.

It's moments like these that your heart and your gut begin whispering among themselves. Your mind then tries to spy in on their conversation, using the neurons up your spine like the string between two cups. *Was there something in that glance?* Your heart says there was, and your gut agrees, so your mind starts analyzing.

I think I found what you've told me about in your story.

Tomatoes

Every time I stand in my kitchen, I'm emotionally abused.

There are twelve tomatoes slouching on the windowsill, unaware of their effect on me. My father was so pleased with himself when he brought them inside from the garden. My mother's cheeks turned red with pride when she saw them. "How lovely," she smiled, showing him my validation, the way all good wives do for their husbands.

But no one in our family eats them, so they sit there and fester and decompose and rot.

I'm at the sink, peeling potatoes for dinner, looking at the tomatoes on the windowsill in front of me, as I'm stripping the potatoes' skin. My mother had asked the way all mothers do: placing her soft hand on my forearm. "The bag is in the fridge."

I stand here, peeling.

Then, you lean over my shoulder and bring with you our memories. Your chest brushes against my back. Our ears glide against each other, the way they used to once before. I hear the slicing sound of our ears. Your stubble numbs my neck. I feel pins and needles there.

I'm back and my mouth goes metallic. I watch the potato skins fling into the metal sink. The peeler slices through the potatoes. It makes a slicing noise. *Sssst.* Hope. *Sssst.* Remorse. *Sssst.* Pain. *Sssst.* Fear. *Sssst.*

And then again, the tomatoes on the window sill.

Why tomatoes?

No one eats tomatoes, except my father.

I usually hardly ever see the tomatoes on the window sill. There were two before, then five the next day, then seventeen. At one point there were twenty-six of them.

Every time I try to enjoy dinner with my family, I can't help but stare at him putting small, fleshy tomatoes into his mouth.

They crush between his teeth without much effort at all. *How was your day?* The skin snaps. *Why did he say that?* My blood runs down his chin. *How did you handle it?* My mother smiles at him and strokes his arm. *Do you think the situation will get any better?* He laughs.

May I be excused?

White Lie

———

The mother of Michael Alexander Baker III had a look of sheer hysteria on her face. Last night's foie gras was clinging to her newly purchased, Italian, ceramic dish and would not come off, despite her exhaustive efforts. Her neatly fixed hair was starting to come loose while she frantically scrubbed the inside of it. Also, she could see her son doing something odd outside as she looked through the window above the sink.

He was grabbing handfuls of dirt and smearing it on his arms and neck and behind his knees. She watched him throw mud directly into his face, uprooting whole clumps of weeds, and flailing his arms so wildly that arcs of pebbles and dirt went flying in every direction. He looked like an ape out there.

Dish soap puffed in the air as she dropped the sponge quickly and ran to the door. She barely rubbed her hands on her apron before grabbing the sliver knob of the door.

"Honey, stop that! Now come inside and wash up at once." She hoped the neighbors had not seen her ballistic child and glanced around to make sure.

He didn't want to, but the sympathetic little boy did as his mother asked and got up to come inside. Teardrops tight-roped along his eyelids as she pulled him into the house.

The following day, after the dish, the bathtub, and her son had all been thoroughly cleaned white, Mrs. Baker drove her son to a playdate at his classmate's house. His name was Paul Loreux. *Must be of French decent,* she thought when she first heard his name. The event had been arranged a few days prior, which Mrs. Baker had neatly written into her calendar. The woman with whom she had spoken with on the phone sounded quite pleasant. Mrs. Baker was more than happy to drive her son over for a social engagement.

Sitting in the passenger seat beside her, Michael had an aromatic pecan pie bouncing in his lap as the car cruised along.

"Are you excited for your playdate," she asked.

"Yes! Very much so!" he beamed at her from beneath frivolous curls of hair. The woman sadly had no one else in the car to turn to and boast about her little boy's impeccable articulation. But hearing it was enough. She'd tell her stylist later about how proper he sounded.

Not too long later, Mrs. Baker knocked on a perfectly quaint front door of a deliciously decorated suburban house, then looked down at her son and smirked happily. She was holding the pie in one hand and her son's tiny hand in the other.

A woman opened the door.

"Why, hello there!" The greeting had a tinge of disrespect for her liking.

"Good evening, I'm looking for a Mrs. Dierdre Loreux."

"And you must be Michael's mother." A thick, ashy hand jutted towards her.

"Paul!" Yells. Runs. The son. His wrist. Grab his wrist! Stop him!

"Come back here, Michael." An order. Escaping. Hugging. Wave your hand. Call him back. Wave at him. He's not looking. Check the street.

"Oh, don't worry about it. Boys will be boys, right?" A chuckle. The pie. Hurry. "This looks delicious, thank you! Would you like to come in?"

"No."

Just go. Car door.

The screech of the tires. Two, black marks on the pavement.

Diedre Loreux kept a disheartening smirk on her face as she closed the door. It was all too familiar.

She walked to the kitchen to place the pie on the counter and could hear the boys laughing in the living room. They were completely oblivious, thank goodness.

Her husband walked in and kissed her hot cheek. "Great looking pie. Who's it from?"

Diedre did not say anything to him. She stood, bracing herself against the counter, with the thought 'He's just a boy. He's only a little boy', echoing in her mind.

Later, as she buttoned his jacket for him, Diedre asked, "Did you enjoy yourself, Michael?"

"Yes, I did very much, Mrs. Loreux. May I come back tomorrow?"

Diedre stopped fixing his coat and looked into his excited blue eyes staring at her. She felt a knot tighten in her chest, seeing his eyes grow wider in anticipation, before lying directly to his tiny, happy face. "Of course you can, baby! You're always welcome here, you know that." The immediate joy that painted his face broke Diedre's heart, but she hid it from him perfectly.

She held his hand gently as they walked to his car where his mother was waiting for him. Diedre opened the back-seat door and Michael bounced in. She could hear his mother already scolding him from the front seat, "Michael, buckle your seat belt."

The door was barely closed before the car lunged away from the sidewalk. She could see Michael's little face beaming at her through the window, hand waving wildly, as they drove off.

Diedre stood at the street long after the car disappeared around the corner. She closed her eyes and said a prayer, asking God to not let that part of him be destroyed.

"Amen."

When she opened her eyes, teardrops were tight-roping on her eyelids.

Seboeis

———

I was walking without a compass in the woods of Maine. I've been going there for years and years and I'm never afraid of getting lost. I actually prefer to get lost. That's the only place I actually feel like I'm not lost.

I would walk along for a while, stop and just listen. I had my gun over my shoulder so I'd always be listening for deer, but sometimes I would just stop to listen.

Eventually, I was making my way west and I came to a dirt road that just 'vsst', ran itself through the middle of the woods.

I popped my head out from the trees. I looked left down that way. I looked right. And there was a rise in the road. I couldn't see over the rise in the road to my right. So I was cautious. Then I stepped out, slowly.

And I'm walking along, walking along, and look up and there's the biggest dog I've ever seen in the middle of the road and I think to myself, 'That's not a dog. It's a wolf!' The biggest son of a bitch you've ever seen. And I look him dead in the eyes and he looks me dead in the eyes. And for a second, I'm nervous.

"You were?"

Absolutely. I put my hand on my gun.

"You did?"

You bet your ass I did. And I just watch him for a second. Just him and me. And he looks at me but I don't move. And I think, "Oh buddy, what are you gonna do, huh?" I stand my ground. If I turn and run he'll start chasing after me and I don't want to do that. So neither of us move. But eventually he hops into the woods and 'ttt ttt ttt' off he goes like he never saw anything. Scared the wits out of me but the most beautiful creature I've ever seen.

Show Me Where It Hurts

———

I had a best friend in high school. Keyword *best*. Keyword *had*.

And we saw each other again tonight after a very long time and you stepped back when you saw me. I knew then not to extend my hand like I've done to every other person I've never cared about in this room, let alone hug you like I used to.

I socialize and ask people what they've been doing with their lives and not listening to a single word because I'm too busy looking over their shoulders at you or wondering where you are and what to ask you.

What have you and I become toward each other? I never betrayed you, right? "What were you saying? Sorry."

Wasn't it *me* sitting beside you, riding through the mountains of New York in your family van, hearing the secrets of your father's condition that your mother wouldn't even tell her own sister? I wouldn't dare tell a soul because I know how much it hurt you to hear. And I know how scared you are to be just like him. I used to listen to the arguments you had with your mother when you were learning to drive but I kept my mouth shut about them and even still keep the stories you told me, just so I know something about you that no one else in the world knows. Even your best friend now doesn't know some of your stories. But I know. And I never said "slow down" or "watch out" from the back seat because your mother did that and you told me how much you hated when she did that. So I just sat in the back seat, watching my brave friend be the first one behind the wheel.

You grew your beard out and you look different and you walked away toward the open bar and never came back to the circle of people we were talking to and I watched you look over, take a depressingly large sip, and turn to find someone else to talk to. Is that seven? Let's talk like we used to as teenagers growing up together, trying to figure the world out. What's wrong?

Don't you mind? I gave you something you could never give back. Never wanted anything back.

And it's a parasite.

I guess I'd tell you about yesterday, when my mother asked me to blow out the candle before we left. But I put the lid on it instead and watched the flame become still and weak, before caving in on itself.

We're just both looking for acceptance and validation in all the wrong places.

I still haven't told you about when I cried to my father.

I left my house at two in the morning for you and all I said when you called me, hysterically crying, was "What's wrong?" And you told me, and then I said, "I'll be right there." That was it. *I'll be right there.* It was two in the morning and it didn't matter. *I'll be right there.*

But that was high school, right? This is now. It can't be like that anymore, can it? And the realization that we changed, in exactly the way I didn't want us to, is crippling. That was us! Remembering it is like a dream so good you keep thinking about it. Like the ones you get to fly in. And you think, I wish that was real! But it was real! We were so inseparable, so incredibly vulnerable without meaning to be. We were like water and the color blue.

Now this is us: Hello, how have you been? Not too bad. Same old, same old.

So much swallower, but I know we're still water. Why are we wading? Let's swim again!

And then I'm back from the dream again. Back to the conversation I'm in, watching you over their shoulder.

I can recall all the numerous, seemingly unimportant details so well. The details that make life what it is. Like that hug when your mom told me she was glad you had me, how you cracked my thumbs watching television, that beer we stole from your uncle's refrigerator to pass between us like a secret, the tree we climbed, Beowulf, American Eagle flip-flops at the height of our humid summers, the green carpet in your living room that held the mold of your hand if you pressed hard enough, your mother's to-do lists we'd wake up to after I spent the night with chores like empty the dishwasher and let the dog out and peel the carrots, and my own spot at the dinner table.

Where the did that all go?

Jack Dunbar

Death is What Bonds Us; or, Buck Fever

―――――

Taking an animal's life is very simple. They are unsuspecting and vulnerable, eating grass as the sun rises.

From the stand in the tree, you're watching the beast and trying to be as quiet as you can so you can shoot it dead. You've never been this close to a wild animal before, so you notice how its legs flex and move its hooves over the leaves and grass of the woods. It has no idea how much longer it has before it dies.

―――――

The thing went right in and dug into the flesh and punctured the lung or the heart and made the deer bleed its same, red blood all over. Suddenly the animal takes off as fast as it can from us, running from the strange vultures sitting in the tree.

"Wow! What a shot. Hit him right in the chest, right where you wanted it to go, directly behind the front knee. Great aim." *Hunting with arrows is tougher than with guns.*

We let the tense atmosphere run away with the injured deer, finally able to speak and exhale and breathe without a problem, climbing down with our strong, working arms.

The terrible part was that we had to basically get on our hands and knees after that and track down our kill that was dying. Every one-hundred yards or so we'd find a tiny dot of red blood on a red autumn leaf, reflecting in the sunlight that was just starting to come through the trees. It was difficult to see the red of the blood against the red of the leaves, but we could always see it. And we'd stare into the trees ahead, knowing we were heading in the right direction.

Eventually we found the deer, but it wasn't dead. It was struggling, laying down, gasping. I could see the light fading from its black, beady eyes. There was a large gash to its neck and chest. Blood pooled there. And its chest was heaving like a bagpipe.

When we finally found it, all I could think about was not how delicious it would be later, after we butchered it. We walked closer and the deer saw man up close for the first time and it became scared and it needed to stand and escape, but it was too weak and too hurt and dying.

To put it out of its misery, I watched the deer watch him take an arrow, place it in the bow and pull back. *You can feel the bow helping you draw the arrow back. It clicks when it's fully drawn back. Here, feel it.* The deer looked on, panicked.

He pressed the tip of the arrow against the deer's neck and released the arrow. It bolted through the animal's neck just as fast as it would if you were releasing it from three-hundred yards away. The arrow pierced through the tough muscles of the animal's neck like it was nothing and sunk into the dirt on the other side.

The deer flailed and kicked and opened its eyes wide and its mouth wide. The legs jerked and kicked. *It's just the reflexes now.* But I knew it wasn't. The animal screamed without any sounds, kicking a few more times, and then it heaved and died right in front of us. No one seemed to care. They stood around, as if waiting for the train. *What did you think about the game Sunday?* I watched the deer take its final breath.

He pulled out a serrated hunter's knife and tore open the flesh on the stomach like a zipper and dumped all the guts onto the leaves the deer had just been fleeing on. The pile of tissue and organs puffed the deer's warm spirit into the early morning air. *The coyotes will have a feast tonight.* They laughed the way jackals do. And it just died.

———

We dragged the deer's dead body out of the woods. The lifeless body hung heavy in my strong, working arms as the hooves dragged over the leaves and grass of the woods.

Café

The Americans had more than one starving organ. After a day of exploring the so-so city of Barcelona, they decided to submit to the aching whelps of their feet and stop at a café for some refreshments and handle at least the stomach.

"This will do, I guess," said one young man, annoyance resounding from his voice. The three people slumped jackets and bags from their shoulders, dropping their things around their feet, without much regard, onto the pavement. Spanish families, having their late afternoon *meriendas*, eyed the raucous people the way cows eye a farmer coming too close, forcing them to stand and move.

One of the Americans pulled a menu swiftly from beneath a cup and saucer, clanking the china noisily and disrupting the neat presentation it was set up in. The families around them scoffed, *¡Qué tanto ruido!* They pulled their plates closer.

"I'm getting sick and tired having to act like a goddamn linguistic scientist just to get a cup of coffee around here," the girl complained. Her eyes scanned the words without reading much. "What the hell is *pie-el-la?*"

"No idea," said one boy.

"Beats me," said the other.

As they sat, trying to decipher the strange words, slick Europeans dashed by. Honeyed sunlight, sticking to the rooftops, oozed down the façade of immaculate Spanish architecture, spilling into the *vía* among the cars. Across the street *La Boquería* flooded with lush Spanish fruit delivered from the countryside this morning. All around them people spoke Spanish and Catalan, sounding like violins: so crisp, effortless, and flowing.

"What do you guys think you're getting," the first boy inquired.

"No idea. I don't even know what the hell I'm looking at," said the other boy.

A timid waitress had been eyeing the three new guests in her section from a table near the back of the patio. It was beneath an awning, pressed against the chin of the *restaurante*. The woman rubbed her palms on her apron, anticipating a cup of water slipping through her sweaty hand and landing on the girl.

"Gabriella, ¿qué haces ahora amiga? Véte ya!," her friend Cristiana inquired. Cristiana was a much more aggressive waitress who wouldn't be as intimidated in such a predicament. She recently had had a baby boy, Jugo Javier, and depended on good tips.

"Acaban de sentarse unos americanos en mi mesa."

"Pues, habla bien tía."

"No hablo inglés bien. Tú lo sabes."

"No te preocupes. Vámonos!"

Gabriella grabbed three glasses of water and slowly stepped through the other tables towards them. Perspiration slid down her back and down the glasses, fighting the heat of the Mediterranean sun overhead.

"Welcome," she said to them in her Spanish accent, trying her best to sound okay. "You'll like to eat?"

The girl rolled her eyes. "Yes, ———— to have s—— to eat, what—," looking at her nametag, "Gabby? I— love —coffee —you ——. Ne—— sugar —more. ——, —, you —want ——?"

Gabriella hadn't understood what the pretty girl had asked her for. The words had come out of her mouth like a dam collapsing. She heard coffee and something else about sugar. She wanted to clarify if the girl wanted *café con azúcar* but didn't want to offend her and didn't know how to ask.

Gabriella watched the girl, waiting for more words, but she didn't keep speaking. The two young men did not seem to want anything. At least it didn't seem like they did from their silence when Gabriella looked at them. She was about to walk away to decipher it all when suddenly one of them began speaking. "— coffee —me ——. Not —water." She nodded to the young man who had spoken up.

"—have a sandwich ————," said the other boy, matter-of-factly.

Sanwiche. She knew that, but what kind? Two coffees. One with something and a *sanwiche*?

"Okay. Un moment." Gabriella could see the Americans scolding her meek English skill and pathetic attempt at its syntax. She walked with as much poise as she could back to the waitress stand feeling like a student who had just spelled a word incorrectly in the championship spelling bee.

"¿Qué pasó?" Cristiana pulled her friend close by the wrist. She had been watching out of the corner of her eye while tending to her own patrons.

"No les entiendí. No sé."

Buckets Full of Roses

———

Grocery stores always have a florist tucked into the corner like hair behind an ear, slapped into the layout by the contractor at the last minute. "Actually, they're important."

While you shop, you keep looking at the flowers playing hide-and-seek between the aisles.

You pass by the *New York Times* with articles about what terrors are happening in the world, and what happened yesterday at the game when they sang the national anthem. You keep that thought in the back of your mind, all the while you keep glancing at the flowers.

Maybe you'll want a bouquet for the kitchen table.

Eventually, you pull your cart out to loop into the aisle with all the drugs and you nearly hit the florist station, just barely missing a pot of orchids. You quickly glance at the person behind the counter, making sure they still haven't seen. Their face is hidden. It's always hidden. They tend to this, mess with that, stick their finger in this pot to feel the moisture, water this, snip that, aggravate the perfectly content flowers. You can only make out the top of their head over the plants or their voice when you ask a question. "Yes, water twice a day and keep out of direct sunlight" or "Those aren't as nice as these."

Stepping back, you take a view of everything: the violets, the babies breath, the hydrangeas, the orchids you nearly just hit, the little, plain green house plants squatting in their pots and…the roses. So many beautiful roses. Red, pink, white, peach, yellow, orange. There are groups of them in plastic buckets sitting on the shelves in front of the florist station.

You've smelled roses before, of course, but it's important to smell them now and stay up to date. *Stop and smell the roses.* The topmost shelf has a bucket of white and pink roses, a few peach are there too. You pull one by the stem, careful not to prick your finger from the thorns and bring it to your nose.

Then the second shelf, and third, smelling your way down to the bottom.

Finally, on the bottom shelf, overpacked in a large bucket, is an array of red roses. Some are lighter cherry colors while others are deeper, more suppressed reds. Merlot, currant, mahogany, and blood red. You pull a rose out and smell it.

"Excuse me, why do roses come in so many different colors if they all smell the same?"

The person moving about behind the counter answers: "Well surely the peach ones smell better than the yellow and those wrinkly, dark red ones down there."

"They all smell the same to me."

"Well, some people have a preference for a certain color."

I See My Reflection and I Turn My Face

―――

I hit him. I couldn't believe I hit him. I still can't believe that I hit him. The sting on my hand is still there. I feel the sting on my hand when I shake everyone else's hands. I can still see the mark on his face. Everyone mistakes it for rosy cheeks. He looks just like me. If only he didn't make me so mad. Maybe, just maybe, I wouldn't have done it. I shouldn't have done it. I couldn't help myself. If the Marines taught me anything it was self-defense. I can't believe I hit him. He's just like me. I hurt him. I hurt them both. I should say I'm sorry. But if the Marines taught me anything it was to keep my feelings to myself. What does she think of me? Does he forgive me? They never say anything when they eat their dinner. But, don't you have to be strict with a son? I still can't believe I hit him. She drinks now. I try not to grimace at her. I really try hard not to, but I can't help it. I can't believe I hit him. Yesterday, I left. I didn't even turn on the radio. I drove. I thought about things. I didn't solve any of my problems. I tried. But I couldn't. I drove to a motel. It was called Motel 7. I can't believe I hit him. I asked for a room. It was twenty-eight dollars. I gave the clerk a fifty. I wonder if he's ever hit his son. I wonder if Grant ever hit his son. Or if Roosevelt ever hit his son. Or if Jefferson ever hit his son. Of if Lincoln ever hit his son. The hotel room was small and cold. The bed was scratchy. I cried for three hours. I wanted to punch the mirror in the bathroom when I looked at myself. I was pathetic. I didn't punch it. I'm never going to touch anything again in my life. There was a neon sign outside the window of my motel room. It flickered across the street. The brightness of the flashing light slapped my face. I pulled the shades as wide was they would go and stood there. I closed my eyes and didn't move for an hour and ten minutes. I let the sign slap me. Then I laid back down on the bed and did it again. After, I walked across the street to the sign and went inside the building underneath it, to the bar. I drank until I couldn't think about it. I cussed at the bar tender. I told him to hit me. I met a girl who told me her name was Rebecca. She slapped me when I tried to kiss her. I wanted more. She left so then I talked to Margaret. She lived in my town. She came back to the hotel room with me. I tried to kiss her, but she told me I was a drunk

130

and that I needed to sleep it off. She was next to me when I woke up this morning. I woke up the next morning and she told me I was pathetic and that I was an asshole and that I needed help. She said I was aggressive and tried to force myself on her and I remembered that she hit me. Since I was rude, she said the least I could do was drive her back to where she lived, so I took her with me. I only turned on the radio because she said she felt awkward sitting in the car with no other noise. I decided as we drove to stop and grab my things and leave. I remember seeing him and smiling at him before walking out the door.

––––––

I was deciding whether or not to take an apple for the road, or if it would remind me of where I came from. I figured the seventy-five dollars I was taking with me, saved up over the last few months, would be enough to get something on the road. Besides, my mother had just gone to the grocery store yesterday and she hated when I ate the food she just bought. "What do you think, money grows on trees or something," I could hear her complaining.

Now, money is always an issue with us. Never used to be, but always would be if I stayed around any longer. I'm sorry but I can't take the sounds of her tears anymore or the sounds of her waiting for Sir to come home.

He left. He's not coming back. Luckily, I remember the smirk he had walking out the front door to his car, some lady sitting in the passenger seat. I wanted to think she was his therapist, but I knew better. I'll always remember the stench of cigar on his ego strutting through the kitchen to the bedroom and the desperate cries of my mother pulling at his arm as he stuffed his suitcase with all his neatly folded clothes.

For some reason, my mother still keeps a framed picture of him on her dresser next to the empty jewelry box with the flowers on it. She showed Mrs. Richardson and Mrs. Sinclair when they came over last week for tea and cookies. "And this was (him) when he was in the Marine Corps back in '78. Wasn't he such a dish?" The other two had giggled together, nodding at his deliciously fake smile. I could see how my mother yearned for the life they thought she had, with an adoring husband and complacent child. Little did they know, his pillow hadn't been slept on in months and she was putting vodka in her tea as she called from the kitchen, "Nancy, two teaspoons of sugar or one?"

At first, it was all fine and dandy. We didn't talk about Sir when he left and it was as if he never even existed to us. But eventually bills started showing up and we couldn't avoid the fact that he was needed.

First, the water bill came. Three-hundred and fifty dollars. So my mother decided to let the lawn brown a little bit instead of wasting every drop to maintain its secret-keeping, emerald green. Then, the car payment. Six-hundred dollars. Goodbye to riding in comfort. She keeps the windows up in summer when she drives, fearing someone might holler from their mailbox, "Evette, drinks at our place tonight! Bring your husband around seven."

Back then, she always went out with her friends and I usually had to wait for her to get off the phone with Abigail Rothenfield before I could call my girlfriend, Nora. They would be talking about all sorts of things. "I heard Georgina found her daughter with that Mullaley boy again the other night. I would give my bottom dollar to see her lose her shit like I heard she did." I'm not dating Nora anymore and she typically stays indoors now, the shades cupped over the house's eyes. It's all because of Sir and that woman.

I want to stay. Honestly, I do. *Who's going to take care of me?* "Don't you worry," Momma told me that time we don't talk about. "He won't do that again." But I can't stand the look my friends give me when she picks me up from school in that shit-box of a car and how often we have to dodge people we know in the bread aisle.

As a last minute decision, I grab the apple and stuff it in my jacket pocket. Maybe the guilt of taking it will force me to come back.

Ten miles later, I walk into the motel's office and ring the small bell sitting on the counter. A man walks out from the room in back.

"What can I do you for?"

"Just one room, please."

"How long?"

"I don't know."

"Hey, you're (his) boy aren't you? You look just like him."

Let Me Bare Arms

―――――

Going to war seems so liberating. Not for all the killings and stuff and having to murder innocent people, but for everything else.

I would not be able to kill anybody, honestly. You hear all those horror stories about watching children blowing up or seeing limbs get torn from their sockets and having to shoot a person and how unbearably hot it is there. The heat would surely kill me. I can't think about it. Let's talk about something else and not that blistering, unbearable heat.

Sometimes you hear veterans reminisce with each other at parties, standing off to the side. You overhear them say stuff to each other and you wonder about what it was like. "I had to put my finger in my buddy's jugular to keep him from bleeding out during my last tour." And you hear their responses to him. "You deserve a metal for that!" or "How's he doing now?" or "You're a brave man!" And they slap each other's backs in quick, masculine affirmations and they take sips of their scotch, silently toasting to the joys of life and being able to return home to the people they love, unharmed.

I wouldn't ever want to touch anyone's blood. To be completely honest, I don't think I could. I'd pass out as soon as I saw it. But maybe being there for them, and seeing the entire thing, I'd be able to do it. But God, I wish I could do that.

Then you think about all the other details of being there: chain-smoking cigarettes, how we'd all be smoking together, walking as a group, keeping an eye on one another. Someone would always have an extra cigarette for you when you run out because you support each other as best as you can over there, making use of whatever the government was giving you. They'd give you a cigarette, knowing you need to dull your senses after just having seen that.

And how your boots would all smell the same when you take them off in the tent because you're all men with working bodies that sweat when they walk for miles in the heat. And being in the tent shirtless, careless and unashamed, letting your hairy chests have a look at everything. You play cards shirtless and you look around at their hairy chests and remember basic training, back when you were all younger and smooth-skinned, when it was tough but easier together, and still together now.

And one by one you'd go take a leak just outside the flap of the tent, out in the open, right there, basically still in the tent. "I know it was fucking terrible," you say, turning around, while everyone can hear the sound of your urine slapping the dirt. They keep talking and thinking, not embarrassed at the sound of your urine slapping the dirt because if you closed your eyes you wouldn't be able to tell who was urinating.

I wouldn't even feel bad vomiting in front of everyone when I see something truly grotesque. I'd just lean over and empty the contents of my stomach onto the dirt, right in front of everyone, letting them see how my stomach rings itself like a sponge. I'd let them hear the grotesque sounds I make when I vomit. I'd stand up with tears running down my cheeks from straining so hard to throw up. And I'd rub my blood shot eyes and the tears from throwing up and say something religious without meaning to, like "Oh, Jesus!" And I'd look at all of them and they'd know and understand me because they were experiencing it too and they wouldn't have to say anything. I'd know they'd understand. Then someone would console me, "I know buddy. It's alright. We got your back." And he'd rub my back and leave his hand on my back and he wouldn't remove his hand so quickly. And I'd look at him with my watery, blood shot eyes from throwing up in front of them all, and I'd be grateful to be there with them and be grateful they were there with me. Then he'd hand me a cigarette.

Plastic Plants

———

...still, I didn't mean anything by what I did. I'm trying to figure myself out as much as you're trying to figure me out, okay. Cut me some slack.

Would this be a good time, between your scoffs and lack of ability to understand, to tell you how it felt later tonight when it would all be thrown back in my face? Or would you rather not hear about that? "I heard you poured out the contents of your heart in that bathroom sink like a water balloon."

"You're drunk. Just go to bed."

I wanted to be respectful, so after you found out what happened between us I wanted to explain myself and discuss it with you. Oh, if you only knew the hurt I did not want to cause anybody to ease the hurt I was hoarding. Selfish, I know and no, it doesn't feel better and I know you don't really care, but I just had to say that.

So here we are: discussing, yelling, being hurt even more, not solving anything.

There's a plant on the table between us.

I touch the leaves and they're all coated with wax. It's strange how you don't know, and you have to make sure.

"Well, I'm sorry you feel that way," I say, stroking the leaf.

I guess we'll never speak again. Must be my fault.

We Would All Be Dead

———

I lounged into a wooden chair with my arm draped over the back of it to watch the sun die. Every time I shifted my weight, the nails whimpered in the chair.

My father had asked for the house to be built facing the East, to be able to see these glorious sunsets in the afternoon from the porch.

I exhaled and watched the radiant sun march off to conquer the darkness beyond the horizon, resplendent in golden cloth, his arms spread wide. It was good and it was beautiful, and I was breathing deep and long.

Inside, the table was being set for dinner and I could hear the plates sliding over the linen. Potbellied, crystal glasses were placed beside the plates. The door was too narrow to see into the kitchen, but I could smell garlic smothered bread.

The sun hadn't set yet, but I was called to come inside and eat.

Things I Told my Therapist

"So where did we leave off? Ah yes, you had an idea about how we're all connected?" Dr. Ian Kavanagh adjusted the glasses on the bridge of his nose as he looked up from the yellow notepad. His patient was sitting on the couch across the room, a very unthreatening man he knew was on the brink of a manic episode.

Almost without missing a beat, the conversation started right where they had left off. "You asked me if I think we're connected but I said I both know and don't know because we're all periwinkles and we know things we don't know yet, somewhere in there, buried in our heads— some call it a curtain, but the point is it's not visible, well not in the sense of seeing with your eyes but with your mind and the meat of the snail is what I don't know, but know, and I don't know how to get to it—do I sing like I used to when I was a kid on the beach, cry, but the point is I know it's there but can't get to it which is why I am where I am or going where I'm going, that's up to you, and what's interesting is that some people have been able to get to it and have come back and shared it and how did they do that?"

"How did they do what, exactly?"

"It reminds me of when someone is staring at you. How do you know?"

Dr. Kavanagh wasn't quite sure what to make of the rambling thought process. He looked at the young man sitting across from him and raised his eyebrows, trying to decipher what he meant.

"That's it! We don't know but we know, and we know because we can sense them, but I bet it goes beyond that to the point when we can sense them all."

"Sense them all meaning all people?"

"Yes. I took a karate class once and they said Chi. Yes, Chi, that's right!"

Dr. Kavanagh looked down to make a note as the ramblings continued.

"Sometimes I think if I concentrate hard enough, I'll figure it out and the neuron will connect and my head will rush into knowledge but it will seem like I'm having a stroke but I'll actually be having a stroke and then I won't be able to talk about it and I'll be muted in enlightenment because life or God or whatever you believe won't let you know and tell and it's like you're creating and perceiving at the same time." There was a moment's silence before he shouted, "The power of the mind!"

"Do you believe in God?"

His face contorted in though before completely disregarding the question, "Have you ever thought about something and came across it later?"

Not thinking twice about being dismissed, as good therapists do, Dr. Kavanagh replied, "Well yes, most certainly."

"I'd think the neuron connecting would be like a stroke and it would be a stroke because it would be like a stroke, at least that's what I'd think, but that's the creating and the perceiving part because it's like the discovery of electricity, this energy I have that I know is there, and the knowledge of how it all works, like leaning over God's shoulder because stuff exists despite whether we know it exists so why can't this be true and obviously the tree makes a sound and the energy of electricity existed before it was discovered, we just had to discover it but it had always been there, same as the stars and the planets and beyond before Galileo and again, creating and experiencing at the same time like Ying Yang or that scene from that movie—maybe we're a periwinkle or we're on some cliff looking out over it like you're God but you're not God but it's like you are—I mean you are the god of your own body—or maybe it's a step to the second floor of your house—you can feel your toes holding your foot on the stair, in reality, but your heel is touching the endless, floating, and you can't go there though because we are the toes, and time and space holds us too tightly to let our heel go down into the vastness to discover it like a black hole— that's a good point, if we go into it we can't ever get back and that must be what losing your mind is and maybe they know everything and it's making them crazy."

Dr. Kavanagh watched intensely, trying to interpret whatever logic was somersaulting in his head.

"I mean how would you know otherwise, right, and maybe the neuron connected and they thought they were going crazy and they went crazy because they thought they were and it took away their ability to cope and be normal because it was just too much— is that enlightenment—like I said, I guess that's why they say geniuses are the most insane and no one can understand them and they can't even understand themselves, like what

I'm doing right now but I'm not saying I'm a genius but both of us know we both know it's true—and there it is again, that energy we can tap into, I'm telling you."

Dr. Kavanagh looked down again to make another note in his notepad. This time, he underlined his scribbled notation with a thick, dark black line with his pen before looking back up.

"Have you ever done drugs, doc?"

Dr. Kavanagh kept his face still, "I can't say that I have, no."

"I haven't because I'd lose my mind, but I think that's why people do drugs though, right? To see it. It only makes sense that you need to pay large prices to see something like that—you want to know how humanity works then you have to give up your liver to be able to see the particles of energy interacting and how connected we are and you have to lose sobriety and your family and your money and your sanity—the people that are on drugs, they can walk up to God's back and look down over his shoulder for a split second and they give up everything to get back there and look at it again and what if the homeless and the druggies and the crazy people are the most enlightened, like I said, and that would be both curious and not curious at all because, I mean, you need to give something, to get something. Ying Yang. So why not your sanity and have you ever thought about why it is savants or people with autism are usually lacking something else—they can't look in your eyes, but they can tell you a thousand things you never knew just like Ying Yang and the balance of life—having to balance out crossing into dystopia, you have to give up something else and I remember once I read that the brain named itself. How crazy is that, but you have to really think about it and realize that it knew its own name and then you think there has to be more it knows that we don't know yet, and if you think longer about it, why do trees and lungs look the same, rivers and arteries and roadways too because they could all look different but still serve the same purpose and work just as well, but there's a reason they resemble each other and that's the energy and it's God because the energy is God that made them look alike, like the beginning of that story, if you believe in that, and again the stair—remember when I talked about the stair—but this time it's the entire staircase, not just the single stair because you can go up from this step to the top of the staircase where you'd be looking out if you were

God or walk down to the bottom step, the electron, but at the end of the day everything is just a stair."

He was nearly panting at this point. Dr. Kavanagh watched him over the brim of his glasses, the notepad resting on the knee of his crossed legs.

"I don't know doc, do I sound crazy to you?"

My Happiness Went Up Your Nose, and All That was Left was Sorrow

-----

"Caring doesn't sometimes lead to misery. It always does." – John Green

We were sleeping when your brother woke us up. He was drunk and high on cocaine. He was banging the cabinets downstairs and talking to himself. I couldn't hear what he was saying but I listened because I was curious and nervous. And I remember him stomping his way up and down the stairs twelve times. He was trying to wrangle the dogs into his bedroom for the night so they could sleep with him and keep him company.

I was lying next to you, listening, and at the same time I was wondering if I could really see myself as part of this family. I was wondering if whether I was truly happy and also I was trying my hardest not to think of the times when you were high on cocaine. You told me before that you had done it twice.

Once at Tim and Maggie's wedding, you did it with your brother off the bumper of a car in the parking lot. And my memory flashed to a photo I saw of you at the wedding when I didn't know if you were happy for them or because you were high. The other photos made me so excited at first because you were cheering over the balcony above the garden just as they walked out together, and I knew how much you loved them, how much you loved their love, how much you wanted their love and how I was being that for you. But afterwards I was sad because I knew that you did that and the photos changed.

I'm not sure if I believe that you've only done it twice.

Before I knew, when I saw you in those photos, I thought to myself: *He looks so goddamn handsome in that tuxedo. I wish I could have been his date.* But I wouldn't have wanted to be there if you were doing that. And I had thought: *maybe one day he'll be the man I see at the end of the alter,* acting like I already knew my future, taking guesses each time my heart leapt for you. But after you told me, I thought: *Why is he smiling that wide?*

"You're so much better than drugs," I said to you during one of our many arguments about it. "No, not better than the people who do them,

141

that's not what I'm saying. You're young and want to try it. But you are so much better than drugs."

Your brother banged around some more downstairs and I didn't want to be awake. In my head it was you downstairs, drunkenly banging around in some fucked up state, trying to wrangle the dogs to bed.

It wasn't you.

Then you got out of bed quietly so you wouldn't wake me. Your knees cracked. And I heard you walk down the carpeted stairs to the sliding door at the deck. I think you let the dogs out. They were being too loud and drooling with excitement, trying to figure out what was going on. The door slid open and the click of the lock when the door slapped the wood of the frame.

"Keep it down." You told him you didn't want him to wake me.

"Ryan, I'm so fucked up right now. I don't even know how I got home."

When you were back in bed, you knew I had woken up. I heard your skin slide across the sheet and you asked me, "Is everything okay?"

I didn't know how to answer.

Lightning Source UK Ltd.
Milton Keynes UK
UKHW011431310521
384684UK00007B/831/J